ST. Croix

TRAVEL GUIDE

2024

Discover the Secrets, Beauty and Culture of this Virgin Island in your Vacation.

Accommodations, Maps and Tourist Attractions also included

Table of Contents

Chapter 1. Welcome to St. Croix

A Brief Introduction to the Island

Welcome to St. Croix, a hidden gem nestled in the heart of the Caribbean Sea, where pristine beaches, lush landscapes, and vibrant culture converge to create a paradise unlike any other. As the largest of the U.S. Virgin Islands, St. Croix beckons with its rich history, diverse ecosystems, and a warm, welcoming spirit that instantly makes you feel at home.

Imagine stepping onto the sun-kissed shores, where the soft whispers of the ocean breeze gently greet you. The turquoise waters glisten under the radiant sun, inviting you to dive in and explore a world teeming with marine life. St. Croix's beaches are not just places to relax—they are gateways to adventure. Whether you're snorkeling among colorful coral reefs at Buck Island, kayaking through the serene Salt River Bay, or simply basking in the tranquility of Sandy Point, each moment here promises to be unforgettable.

Beyond its natural beauty, St. Croix is a tapestry of history and culture. Walk through the charming streets of Christiansted and Frederiksted, where colonial architecture tells tales of the island's storied past. These towns are alive with history, from the imposing Fort Christiansvaern, which has stood guard over Christiansted Harbor since the 18th century, to the vibrant markets where the island's heritage is celebrated daily through art, music, and local cuisine.

St. Croix's cultural richness is further reflected in its festivals and traditions. Time your visit to coincide with the Crucian Christmas Festival, a jubilant celebration filled with music, dance, and colorful parades that highlight the island's unique blend of African, European, and Caribbean influences. As you immerse yourself in these festivities, you'll discover the true heart of St. Croix—its people. Friendly and full of life, the locals are always ready to share a story, offer a smile, or invite you to join in their celebrations.

Cuisine in St. Croix is a delightful journey in itself. Savor the flavors of traditional dishes like kallaloo, a savory stew bursting with local greens and seafood, or indulge in the island's famous rum, crafted with care and tradition at local distilleries. Every meal is an opportunity to experience the island's culinary heritage and the fresh, vibrant ingredients that define its food.

In St. Croix, every corner you turn reveals something new and exciting. It's a place where the past and present blend seamlessly, where nature's beauty is ever-present, and where every visitor is welcomed with open arms. So, let the island's enchantment sweep you off your feet and embark on a journey that promises to be as memorable as it is magical. Welcome to St. Croix, your Caribbean adventure awaits.

Why Choose St. Croix?

Why choose St. Croix for your next vacation? The answer is simple: St. Croix is a paradise that promises an unparalleled experience, blending natural beauty, rich culture, and unforgettable adventures. From the moment you arrive, you'll find yourself enveloped by the island's enchanting allure, a place where every day feels like a dream come true.

Imagine waking up to the sound of gentle waves lapping against the shore, the sun casting a golden glow over the pristine beaches. St. Croix's stunning coastlines are perfect for those seeking relaxation or adventure. Whether you're a beach lover eager to lounge on the soft sands of Rainbow Beach, an explorer ready to dive into the vibrant underwater world of the Frederiksted Pier, or a sailor navigating the crystal-clear waters, St. Croix offers something for everyone.

But the island's appeal goes beyond its natural beauty. St. Croix is steeped in history, offering a unique glimpse into its past. Wander through the historic streets of Christiansted and Frederiksted, where the echoes of colonial times resonate through the well-preserved architecture and historic landmarks. Visit the Estate Whim Plantation Museum to step back in time and understand the island's sugar plantation era, or explore Fort Frederik, a symbol of resilience and a window into the island's colonial heritage.

Culture thrives on this vibrant island, with a blend of African, European, and Caribbean influences creating a rich tapestry of traditions, music, and art. Join in the festivities of the annual Crucian Christmas Festival, a lively celebration that showcases the island's unique cultural heritage through colorful parades, music, and dance. Engage with the local artisans at the various markets and galleries, where the creativity of St. Croix's people comes to life in exquisite crafts and artworks.

Culinary delights await you at every corner. St. Croix is a food lover's paradise, offering a tantalizing array of flavors. Indulge in the local cuisine, where fresh seafood, tropical fruits, and traditional dishes like conch fritters and johnnycakes are sure to satisfy your palate. Don't miss the opportunity to visit the island's renowned rum distilleries, where you can sample world-class rums and learn about the island's rum-making history.

St. Croix is also a haven for adventure seekers. Hike through the lush trails of the rainforest, kayak through the bioluminescent waters of Salt River Bay, or embark on a horseback riding tour along the beach. Each adventure offers a new perspective on the island's diverse landscapes and natural wonders.

Choosing St. Croix means embracing a slower pace of life, where every moment is savored, and every experience is treasured. The island's warm and welcoming people, its breathtaking scenery, and its rich cultural heritage combine to create a destination that feels both familiar and extraordinary.

So, why choose St. Croix? Because here, you'll find not just a vacation, but a journey of discovery, relaxation, and joy. Welcome to St. Croix, where your perfect getaway begins.

Chapter 2. Planning Your Trip

When to Visit: Weather and Seasons

Timing your visit to St. Croix can make your experience all the more magical. This Caribbean gem boasts a tropical climate, ensuring warm, inviting weather year-round, but understanding the nuances of its seasons can help you plan the perfect trip.

The Ideal Time: December to April

For many, the best time to visit St. Croix is from December to April. During these months, the island basks in its dry season, offering sunny days, cooler evenings, and a gentle breeze that makes outdoor activities delightful. Temperatures typically range from the mid-70s to the mid-80s Fahrenheit (24-30°C), creating the perfect setting for lounging on the beach, exploring historical sites, or embarking on water adventures.

This period also coincides with the island's vibrant festive season. The Crucian Christmas Festival, running from late December to early January, is a highlight, filling the air with music, dance, and joyful celebrations. It's a time when the island comes alive with cultural events and parades, providing an immersive experience of St. Croix's rich heritage.

The Green Season: May to November

Visiting St. Croix from May to November, also known as the green season, offers its own unique charm. During these months, the island experiences occasional showers, which transform the landscape into a lush, green paradise. The rain is typically brief and often followed by sunshine, keeping your plans mostly uninterrupted.

Temperatures during this season range from the mid-70s to the high 80s Fahrenheit (24-31°C), and the atmosphere is a bit more humid. This is a fantastic time for nature enthusiasts, as the rainforests are at their most vibrant, and the botanical gardens flourish with tropical blooms. The green season is also less crowded, offering a more tranquil experience and the chance to enjoy the island's beauty at a leisurely pace.

Hurricane Season Awareness

It's important to note that the green season overlaps with the Atlantic hurricane season, which runs from June to November. While the risk of a hurricane directly impacting St. Croix is relatively low, it's wise to stay informed and consider travel insurance for peace of mind. Local businesses and hotels are well-prepared for this season, and up-to-date weather information is readily available to help you plan your activities.

Special Events and Wildlife

No matter when you visit, there are special events and natural phenomena to enjoy. From February to March, humpback whales migrate through the waters around St. Croix, offering an unforgettable sight for whale watchers. In July, the Mango Melee celebrates the island's love for this delicious fruit with tastings, contests, and family fun.

In essence, St. Croix is a year-round destination, with each season offering its own distinctive allure. Whether you're drawn to the festive, sunny days of the dry season or the lush, serene beauty of the green season, St. Croix promises an enchanting escape filled with unforgettable memories. Let the island's rhythms guide you to the perfect time for your visit, ensuring a truly magical experience.

How to Get There: Flights and Ferries

Getting to St. Croix is the first step in your adventure to this Caribbean paradise. The journey is part of the excitement, and with a few helpful tips, you'll find yourself on the island's sun-kissed shores in no time.

By Air: Direct and Connecting Flights

The most common way to reach St. Croix is by air, landing at the **Henry E. Rohlsen Airport (STX)**, located just a short drive from the island's main towns of Christiansted and Frederiksted. This modern airport serves as a gateway to paradise, welcoming visitors from around the world.

Direct Flights: Several major airlines offer direct flights to St. Croix from the U.S. mainland. If you're flying from major cities like Miami, Fort Lauderdale, or Atlanta, you can often find convenient non-stop options. These flights typically take about 2.5 to 3.5 hours, whisking you away from the hustle and bustle of city life to the tranquil beauty of St. Croix.

Connecting Flights: If you're traveling from other parts of the U.S. or internationally, you'll likely have a connecting flight through a larger hub like Miami, Atlanta, or San Juan, Puerto Rico. San Juan is a particularly popular connecting point, with frequent flights to St. Croix that are just a quick hop away, taking about 30 minutes.

By Sea: Ferries and Private Boats

For those who love the romance of the sea, arriving by ferry or private boat is a fantastic alternative. While there are no direct ferry services from the U.S. mainland to St. Croix, you can reach the island from nearby locales.

Ferry from St. Thomas: If you're exploring multiple Virgin Islands, you might start your journey on St. Thomas. From there, you can take a scenic ferry ride to St. Croix. The ferry operates several times a week, offering a picturesque 2-hour voyage across the Caribbean waters. Be sure to check the schedule in advance, as services may vary based on the season and weather conditions.

Private Boats and Yachts: For the truly adventurous, sailing into St. Croix on a private boat or yacht is an unforgettable experience. The island's harbors, including Christiansted Harbor and Frederiksted Pier, are well-equipped to welcome maritime travelers. You'll find modern facilities and friendly staff ready to assist you with docking and any needs you might have upon arrival.

Practical Tips for Travelers

- Booking in Advance: Flights to St. Croix can fill up quickly, especially during peak travel seasons (December to April). Booking your flights well in advance ensures you get the best options and prices.

- Travel Documents: As a U.S. territory, St. Croix does not require a passport for U.S. citizens, but bringing one can be useful if you plan to visit nearby international destinations.

- Local Transportation: Upon arrival, you can easily find taxis, rental cars, and even local buses to get you from the airport or ferry dock to your accommodation. Consider renting a car if you plan to explore the island extensively.

The Journey Begins

No matter how you choose to arrive, the journey to St. Croix is part of the adventure. As your plane descends over the turquoise waters or your ferry approaches the island's lush coastline, you'll feel a sense of excitement and anticipation. The beauty of St. Croix awaits, ready to enchant you with its stunning landscapes, vibrant culture, and warm hospitality. Welcome to paradise—your unforgettable island experience starts the moment you set foot on St. Croix.

Travel Essentials: What to Pack

Packing for a trip to St. Croix is an exciting prelude to your adventure in this Caribbean paradise. With its warm climate, vibrant culture, and diverse activities, ensuring you have the right essentials will enhance your experience. Here's a guide to what you'll need to pack for a perfect stay on the island.

Clothing: Light and Breezy

St. Croix's tropical weather means you'll want to pack light, breathable clothing. Think comfort and versatility to keep you cool during the day and stylish for evening outings.

- Beachwear: Swimsuits, cover-ups, and flip-flops are must-haves for beach days. Consider packing a few extra swimsuits so you always have a dry one ready.

- Daytime Attire: Light cotton or linen shorts, t-shirts, tank tops, and sundresses are perfect for daytime activities. Don't forget a wide-brimmed hat and sunglasses to protect you from the sun.

- Evening Wear: Casual yet stylish outfits for dining out or enjoying the nightlife. Lightweight dresses, button-down shirts, and nice shorts or skirts work well.

- Active Wear: If you plan on hiking, kayaking, or engaging in other outdoor activities, bring moisture-wicking activewear and sturdy, comfortable shoes.

Sun Protection: Shield Yourself

The Caribbean sun can be intense, so packing sun protection is essential to keep your skin safe and your vacation enjoyable.

- Sunscreen: A high-SPF, water-resistant sunscreen is a must. Remember to reapply throughout the day, especially after swimming.

- Sun Hat and Sunglasses: A wide-brimmed hat will protect your face and neck, while UV-protection sunglasses will shield your eyes.

- Aloe Vera or After-Sun Lotion: Useful for soothing any accidental sunburns.

Essentials for the Beach and Water Activities

Whether you're lounging on the beach or exploring underwater worlds, these items will ensure you're well-prepared.

- Beach Bag: A roomy, sand-proof bag to carry your essentials to and from the beach.

- Snorkeling Gear: While you can rent gear on the island, bringing your own mask and snorkel ensures a comfortable fit and familiarity.

- Towel and Waterproof Bag: A quick-dry towel and a waterproof bag for wet items and valuables.

Health and Safety: Be Prepared

Ensuring you have basic health and safety items will keep you comfortable and secure during your travels.

- Medications: Bring any prescription medications you need, along with a small first-aid kit containing band-aids, antiseptic wipes, and pain relievers.

- Insect Repellent: Essential for evening outings and visits to natural areas to protect against mosquito bites.

- Hand Sanitizer and Face Masks: Handy for maintaining hygiene, especially in public spaces.

Tech and Gadgets: Capture and Stay Connected

Capture the beauty of St. Croix and stay connected with these tech essentials.

- Camera: A good quality camera or a smartphone with a great camera to capture stunning island vistas.

- Chargers and Power Bank: Keep your devices charged for those long beach days and excursions.

- Waterproof Phone Case: Perfect for taking photos and videos while snorkeling or kayaking.

Travel Documents and Money: Essentials

Ensure a smooth travel experience by keeping your important documents and funds organized.

- Identification: A valid ID or passport (especially useful if you plan to visit nearby international destinations).

- Travel Insurance: Copies of your travel insurance policy for peace of mind.

- Credit Cards and Cash: While credit cards are widely accepted, having some cash is useful for smaller purchases and tipping.

The Little Things: Comfort and Convenience

These small items can make a big difference in your comfort and convenience.

- Reusable Water Bottle: Stay hydrated throughout the day, especially in the tropical heat.

- Books or E-Reader: For those lazy beach days or quiet evenings.

- Small Backpack or Daypack: For carrying your essentials during day trips and excursions.

Ready for Adventure?

Packing thoughtfully ensures you're ready to embrace every moment on St. Croix. As you fill your suitcase with these essentials, you're not just preparing for a trip—you're setting the stage for an unforgettable adventure. With the right gear and a sense of excitement, your time on this beautiful island will be nothing short of extraordinary. Welcome to St. Croix, where paradise awaits!

Chapter 3. Getting Around

Transportation Options: Taxis, Buses, and Car Rentals

Getting around St. Croix is a delightful part of your adventure, offering you the freedom to explore the island's diverse landscapes and vibrant culture. From the ease of taxis to the local charm of buses and the independence of car rentals, there are various ways to navigate this Caribbean paradise.

Taxis: Convenience and Comfort

Taxis are a convenient and comfortable way to travel around St. Croix, especially if you prefer not to drive. You'll find taxis readily available at the Henry E. Rohlsen Airport, major hotels, and popular tourist spots.

- Fixed Rates: Unlike many places where taxis use meters, St. Croix operates on a fixed-rate system. This means you'll know the fare in advance, whether you're heading to the beach, a restaurant, or exploring the island's historical sites.

- Shared Rides: Often, taxis operate as shared rides, especially for popular routes. This can be a great way to meet fellow travelers and save on costs.

- Guided Tours: Many taxi drivers also offer guided tours, sharing their local knowledge and insights as they take you to key attractions. It's like having a personal tour guide with the added benefit of door-to-door service.

Buses: Local Charm and Budget-Friendly

For a taste of local life and a budget-friendly option, consider taking the bus. The Vitran Bus Service operates across the island, providing an authentic experience of St. Croix's daily rhythms.

- Routes and Schedules: Buses run on several routes connecting key towns and villages. While the schedules can be less predictable than in some places, they offer a unique way to see the island and interact with locals.

- Affordable Travel: Bus fares are inexpensive, making this a cost-effective way to get around, especially if you're planning to stay on the main routes.

- Local Experience: Riding the bus gives you a glimpse into everyday life on St. Croix, adding a layer of authenticity to your visit. Don't be shy to ask locals for tips on where to get off or how to navigate the routes—they're often happy to help.

Car Rentals: Freedom to Explore

Renting a car is one of the best ways to explore St. Croix at your own pace. With a rental car, you can venture off the beaten path, discovering hidden beaches, scenic viewpoints, and quaint villages at your leisure.

- Rental Agencies: You'll find several car rental agencies at the airport and in major towns. It's advisable to book in advance, especially during peak tourist seasons.

- Driving Tips: Remember, driving in St. Croix follows the U.S. Virgin Islands' rule of driving on the left side of the road. Take it slow, especially around curves and in unfamiliar areas. Road signs and speed limits are similar to those in the mainland U.S., making navigation straightforward.

- Exploring the Island: With a car, you can easily visit the island's diverse attractions—from the rainforests in the west to the historical sites in Christiansted and Frederiksted, and the serene beaches in between. It's the ultimate way to experience the full beauty of St. Croix.

Practical Tips for Getting Around

- Navigation: GPS and maps are very useful, though asking locals for directions can also lead to delightful discoveries.

- Parking: Most attractions and beaches have ample parking, but in busier areas, be prepared to walk a short distance.

- Safety: St. Croix is generally safe, but it's always wise to take standard precautions. Lock your car, don't leave valuables visible, and be mindful of your surroundings.

Whether you choose the convenience of taxis, the local charm of buses, or the freedom of car rentals, getting around St. Croix adds to the joy of your adventure. Each mode of transport offers its own unique perspective on the island, helping you uncover the many layers of this Caribbean jewel. So, set off with an open heart and a spirit of exploration, ready to experience all that St. Croix has to offer.

Touring St Croix with QR code Maps, how to use the Map.

QR code maps offer several advantages over traditional paper maps, making them a convenient and efficient tool for navigating St Croix. One key advantage is the ability to input your direct location and have the map direct you from your current location to the desired destination. This feature eliminates the need to manually plot out routes and ensures accurate and real-time navigation.

Additionally, QR code maps provide detailed information for each location, including addresses and phone numbers, which can be accessed by simply scrolling down after scanning the code. This eliminates the hassle of searching for contact information separately and streamlines the planning process.

Furthermore, if you prefer to view photos of any location before visiting, QR code maps have you covered. After scanning the map, simply scroll down until you see the photos icon, and then click on it to access a gallery of images showcasing the location's features and amenities.

Now, let's learn how to scan the QR code with your device:

1. Ensure you have a QR code scanner app: If you don't already have one, download a QR code scanner app from your device's app store. There are many free options available for both iOS and Android devices.

2. Open the QR code scanner app: Launch the QR code scanner app on your device. You'll typically find it on your home screen or in your app drawer.

3. Position your device: Hold your device steady and position the camera so that it's facing the QR code. Make sure the QR code is well-lit and within the frame of the camera.

4. Scan the QR code: Once your device recognizes the QR code, it will automatically scan it and provide a prompt or notification with the information embedded in the code.

5. Access the map: After scanning the QR code, you'll be directed to the map interface, where you can input your location, find directions, view contact information, and browse photos of each location.

By following these simple steps, you can easily scan QR code maps with your device and access valuable information to enhance your travel experience in St Croix.

Chapter 4. Where to Stay

Luxury Resorts and Hotels

Choosing where to stay in St. Croix is an integral part of your island experience, and for those seeking luxury and indulgence, the island boasts an array of exquisite resorts and hotels that promise unparalleled comfort and relaxation.

Seaside Splendor: Oceanfront Retreats

Imagine waking up to the gentle sound of waves caressing the shore, with panoramic views of the Caribbean Sea greeting you each morning. St. Croix's luxury resorts offer idyllic oceanfront settings, where every moment is a serene escape into paradise.

The Buccaneer:

 Nestled on a private estate stretching across 340 acres, The Buccaneer is a historic luxury resort that blends old-world charm with modern amenities. From elegant rooms and suites to private villas with stunning sea views, every accommodation option promises luxury and comfort. Indulge in rejuvenating spa treatments, tee off at the 18-hole golf course, or simply lounge by the pool overlooking the turquoise waters.

The Palms at Pelican Cove

 Located on a secluded stretch of beach near Christiansted, The Palms at Pelican Cove offers a tranquil retreat surrounded by lush gardens and crystal-clear waters. Each room and suite features Caribbean-inspired decor, spacious balconies or patios, and easy access to the beach. Enjoy delicious island cuisine at the beachfront restaurant, unwind with a cocktail at the bar, or take a refreshing dip in the infinity pool overlooking the sea.

Historic Elegance: Colonial Charm

For those enchanted by history and colonial architecture, St. Croix's historic hotels offer a unique blend of past and present, where every corner tells a story of the island's rich heritage.

Hotel Caravelle:

 Situated in the heart of Christiansted, Hotel Caravelle is a charming boutique hotel that captures the essence of St. Croix's colonial past. Stay in beautifully appointed rooms and suites adorned with traditional Caribbean furnishings and modern comforts. Step outside to explore the cobblestone streets, historic sites like Fort Christiansvaern, and vibrant waterfront dining options just moments away.

Company House Hotel

 Located in Christiansted's historic district, Company House Hotel offers guests a glimpse into the island's Danish colonial history. This intimate hotel features stylish rooms and suites with contemporary amenities, blending modern comforts with old-world charm.

Wander through nearby galleries, shops, and restaurants, or relax on the hotel's rooftop terrace with sweeping views of the town and harbor.

Luxury Villas: Private Retreats

For those seeking privacy and exclusivity, St. Croix offers a selection of luxurious villas and vacation rentals, ideal for families, groups, or couples looking to escape into their own secluded paradise.

Cane Bay Villa

 Perched above the serene waters of Cane Bay, this luxurious villa offers panoramic ocean views, spacious living areas, and private infinity pools. Ideal for families or groups, the villa features modern amenities, gourmet kitchens, and outdoor living spaces perfect for alfresco dining and sunset cocktails.

Gallows Point Villa

 Located on the southwest coast near Frederiksted, Gallows Point Villa offers a secluded retreat with breathtaking views of the Caribbean Sea and nearby islands. Each villa is beautifully appointed with luxurious furnishings, private terraces, and direct access to secluded beaches. Enjoy the ultimate in privacy and relaxation, with personalized concierge services and access to exclusive amenities.

Unforgettable Experiences: Beyond Accommodation

Beyond luxurious accommodations, St. Croix's resorts and hotels offer a wealth of experiences to enhance your island getaway.

- Water Sports and Activities: Dive into adventure with snorkeling, kayaking, paddleboarding, and sailing excursions offered by resort facilities.

- Fine Dining: Indulge in gourmet dining experiences showcasing fresh seafood, Caribbean flavors, and international cuisine, often paired with stunning ocean views.

- Wellness and Spa: Rejuvenate your body and mind with luxurious spa treatments, yoga sessions on the beach, and wellness programs designed to promote relaxation and holistic well-being.

Embrace Luxury in Paradise

Whether you're drawn to oceanfront elegance, colonial charm, or the seclusion of a private villa, St. Croix's luxury resorts and hotels promise an unforgettable stay immersed in beauty, comfort, and unparalleled hospitality. Each property invites you to unwind, explore, and create cherished memories against the backdrop of this breathtaking Caribbean island. Welcome to a world where luxury meets paradise— welcome to St. Croix.

Chapter 5. Top Attractions

Beaches: The Best Spots for Sun and Sand

St. Croix is a beach lover's dream, offering a diverse array of sandy shores that cater to every kind of sun seeker. Whether you crave the solitude of a hidden cove, the vibrant energy of a bustling beach, or the adventure of underwater exploration, the island's beaches promise unforgettable experiences. Here are some of the best spots to soak up the sun and sink your toes into the sand.

Sandy Point National Wildlife Refuge: A Pristine Paradise

 Sandy Point is one of the longest and most beautiful beaches in the Caribbean. This pristine, two-mile stretch of white sand is a protected wildlife refuge, known for its nesting sea turtles and untouched natural beauty. Open only on weekends and certain times of the year to protect the wildlife, it's the perfect spot for a tranquil escape. Remember to bring everything you need for the day, as there are no facilities on-site. Walking along this stunning shoreline, with nothing but the sound of the waves and the call of seabirds, feels like stepping into a postcard.

71 Route 63, Frederiksted, St Croix 00840, US Virgin Islands

Rainbow Beach: Vibrant and Family-Friendly

 Located just north of Frederiksted, Rainbow Beach is a lively spot popular with both locals and tourists. With its soft sand, calm waters, and colorful beach bar, it's ideal for families and those looking to enjoy water sports. Rent a jet ski, try paddleboarding, or simply float in the gentle surf. The lively atmosphere and amenities make it a great place to spend the whole day. Don't miss the vibrant sunsets, which paint the sky in hues of orange and pink, creating a perfect end to your beach day.

William, St Croix 00840, US Virgin Islands

Cane Bay: A Diver's Delight

 Cane Bay is famous for its incredible snorkeling and diving opportunities. The Cane Bay Wall, a dramatic drop-off located just 200 yards from shore, is a must-visit for divers of all levels. The beach itself is beautiful, with clear, calm waters ideal for swimming and snorkeling.

Rent your gear from one of the nearby dive shops and explore the vibrant underwater world, home to colorful coral reefs, tropical fish, and even the occasional sea turtle. After your aquatic adventures, relax at one of the beachside restaurants, enjoying fresh seafood and a cold drink as you watch the waves.

La Vallee, St Croix 00851, US Virgin Islands

55

Shoy's Beach: Secluded and Serene

For a more secluded experience, head to Shoy's Beach, located near the Buccaneer Resort. This hidden gem is accessible via a short walk through a shady grove, emerging onto a stunning crescent of golden sand. The calm, clear waters are perfect for swimming, and the serene setting makes it an ideal spot for a peaceful picnic.

Bring your own snacks and drinks, as there are no facilities, and enjoy a quiet day in this beautiful, less-crowded spot.

Buck Island Reef National Monument: An Underwater Wonderland

A visit to St. Croix wouldn't be complete without a trip to Buck Island. Accessible only by boat, this uninhabited island is home to one of the finest marine gardens in the Caribbean. The island's white sandy beaches are perfect for sunbathing and relaxing, while the underwater trail at Turtle Beach offers an unforgettable snorkeling experience.

Explore the vibrant coral reefs and swim alongside a myriad of tropical fish in crystal-clear waters. Several tour operators offer day trips to Buck Island, providing everything you need for a perfect beach day in this protected paradise.

Isaac Bay: Off the Beaten Path

 For the adventurous, Isaac Bay offers an off-the-beaten-path experience. This remote beach, located on the easternmost point of the island, requires a bit of a hike to reach, but the effort is well worth it. The untouched beauty of Isaac Bay, with its golden sands and turquoise waters, is a reward in itself.

The beach is perfect for snorkeling, with vibrant coral reefs just offshore. Pack plenty of water and snacks, as there are no facilities, and enjoy a day of solitude and natural beauty.

Chenay Bay: Relaxed and Scenic

Chenay Bay is a relaxed, family-friendly beach with calm waters ideal for swimming and kayaking. The nearby Chenay Bay Beach Resort offers amenities such as chair rentals, a beachfront restaurant, and water sports equipment. The scenic bay is also great for snorkeling, with a variety of marine life to discover. The gentle slope and warm, shallow waters make it perfect for kids and those looking to enjoy a leisurely day by the sea.

St. Croix's beaches offer something for everyone, from lively, activity-filled spots to secluded, tranquil escapes. Each beach has its own unique charm and beauty, inviting you to unwind, explore, and create lasting memories. So grab your sunscreen, pack your beach bag, and set out to discover the sun-soaked shores of St. Croix, where your perfect beach awaits. **Welcome to paradise!**

Historical Landmarks

St. Croix is a treasure trove of history, where the past comes alive through its well-preserved landmarks and stories. From colonial forts to sugar plantations, exploring these historical sites offers a fascinating glimpse into the island's rich and diverse heritage. Here are some of the must-visit historical landmarks that will transport you back in time and deepen your appreciation for St. Croix's storied past.

Fort Christiansvaern: Guardian of Christiansted

Dominating the waterfront of Christiansted, Fort Christiansvaern is a beautifully preserved 18th-century Danish fort that stands as a testament to St. Croix's colonial history. Built between

1738 and 1749 to protect the town from pirates and other invaders, the fort offers a compelling insight into the island's past.

- Explore the Bastions: Wander through the fort's sturdy bastions, cannons poised over the harbor, and imagine the defensive battles that once took place here.

- Historical Exhibits: Inside, the fort houses exhibits detailing the history of St. Croix, from its indigenous inhabitants to its role in the transatlantic slave trade.

- Stunning Views: Climb to the top of the fort for panoramic views of Christiansted and the sparkling Caribbean Sea, a reminder of the strategic importance of this historic stronghold.

P7WX+Q7G, Hospital St, Christiansted, St Croix 00820, US Virgin Islands

Estate Whim Plantation Museum: A Glimpse into Plantation Life

 The Estate Whim Plantation Museum offers an evocative look into the island's sugar plantation era. This restored 18th-century estate is the only sugar plantation museum in the Virgin Islands and provides a vivid portrayal of plantation life during colonial times.

- The Great House: Tour the elegantly furnished Great House, which has been meticulously restored to reflect the lifestyle of the plantation owners.

- The Windmill: Visit the iconic windmill, one of the largest and best-preserved examples in the Caribbean, which played a crucial role in sugar production.

- Slave Quarters: Reflect on the lives of the enslaved people who worked on the plantation by visiting the original slave quarters and learning about their experiences through informative displays and artifacts.

52 Estate Whim, 00840, United States, Frederiksted, St Croix, US Virgin Islands

Phone contact: +13407720598

Fort Frederik: Defender of Freedom

Located in Frederiksted, Fort Frederik is another impressive Danish fortification with a significant place in history. Built between 1752 and 1760, this red-brick fort is not only an architectural marvel but also a symbol of freedom.

- Emancipation Site: Fort Frederik is famously known as the site where enslaved Africans were declared free on July 3, 1848. This momentous event is commemorated each year with Emancipation Day celebrations.

- Cultural Exhibits: The fort now serves as a museum showcasing cultural and historical exhibits, including artifacts from the plantation era and artworks by local artists.

- Scenic Surroundings: Stroll around the fort's grounds, which offer beautiful views of the sea and the charming town of Frederiksted.

Christiansted National Historic Site: A Walk Through Time

 The Christiansted National Historic Site encompasses several historic buildings and structures that capture the essence of the town's colonial past. This site is a must-visit for history enthusiasts wanting to delve deeper into St. Croix's Danish heritage.

- The Scale House: Start your tour at the Scale House, where goods were weighed and taxed during the island's bustling trading days.

- Customs House: Explore the Customs House, an architectural gem that handled all imports and exports in the 18th century.

- The Danish West India & Guinea Company Warehouse: Visit this historic warehouse, which now houses a museum with exhibits on the island's commercial history and the transatlantic slave trade.

Location: 1 Company St, Christiansted, St Croix 00820, US Virgin Islands

The Steeple Building: From Church to Museum

 One of Christiansted's most distinctive landmarks, the Steeple Building, was originally built as a Lutheran Church in the mid-18th century. This iconic structure now serves as a museum, offering a unique glimpse into the island's religious and cultural history.

- Architectural Beauty: Admire the building's striking architecture, including its tall steeple, which has become a symbol of Christiansted.

- Historical Exhibits: Inside, the museum features exhibits on St. Croix's history, including religious artifacts, colonial-era furnishings, and displays on the island's diverse cultural heritage.

St. George Village Botanical Garden: Nature and History Combined

While primarily known for its stunning array of tropical plants, the St. George Village Botanical Garden is also a site of historical significance. Located on the ruins of a 19th-century sugarcane plantation and village, it offers a fascinating blend of natural beauty and historical intrigue.

- Plantation Ruins: Wander through the garden's lush pathways to discover the remnants of the plantation's Great House, factory, and worker's quarters.

- Historical Displays: The garden's museum features exhibits on the island's botanical and agricultural history, providing context for the ruins and the plants you see.

- Living History: Experience living history through the garden's ongoing preservation efforts and educational programs that celebrate St. Croix's natural and cultural heritage.

Location: 1 Company St, Christiansted, St Croix 00820, US Virgin Islands

Phone Contact: +13407731460

Exploring St. Croix's historical landmarks is a journey through time, offering profound insights into the island's rich and multifaceted history. Each site tells a story, from colonial fortresses and grand plantation houses to poignant reminders of the struggles for freedom and equality. As you visit these remarkable landmarks, you'll gain a deeper understanding of the events and people that have shaped this beautiful island, making your stay in St. Croix not only enjoyable but also enlightening. Welcome to a place where history lives on in every corner, waiting to be discovered.

Adventure Activities: Diving, Snorkeling, and More

St. Croix is an adventurer's paradise, offering a myriad of thrilling activities that showcase the island's natural beauty both above and below the water. Whether you're an experienced diver, a snorkeling enthusiast, or a thrill-seeker looking for new challenges, St. Croix has something to ignite your sense of adventure. Here are some of the top adventure activities that will make your island experience unforgettable.

Diving: Explore the Underwater Wonders

St. Croix is renowned for its world-class diving sites, where crystal-clear waters reveal vibrant coral reefs, diverse marine life, and fascinating underwater landscapes.

- Cane Bay Wall: One of the most famous dive sites in the Caribbean, Cane Bay Wall is a spectacular drop-off that begins just a few hundred yards from shore. Descend into the depths to explore an underwater cliff teeming with colorful corals, sponges, and an array of marine species, from parrotfish and barracuda to sea turtles and stingrays.

- Frederiksted Pier: This iconic dive site offers an incredible underwater experience, with the pier's pilings encrusted in corals and sponges, creating a haven for marine life. Night dives at the pier reveal nocturnal creatures like octopuses, lobsters, and seahorses, adding a magical dimension to your adventure.

- Salt River Canyon: Dive into the deep canyons of Salt River Bay, where you can explore dramatic underwater terrain, swim through coral-covered canyons, and encounter large pelagic species like sharks and rays. The area is also historically significant, with remnants of ancient underwater structures.

Snorkeling: Discover Vibrant Reefs

For those who prefer to stay closer to the surface, snorkeling in St. Croix offers an equally captivating glimpse into the island's marine ecosystems.

- Buck Island Reef National Monument: A must-visit for snorkelers, Buck Island is home to an underwater trail that guides you through vibrant coral gardens teeming with tropical fish. The island's protected status ensures that the reefs remain pristine and full of life, making it an unforgettable snorkeling experience.

- Shoy's Beach: This secluded beach near Christiansted is not only perfect for relaxation but also offers excellent snorkeling opportunities. Swim out to the coral reefs just offshore and encounter a variety of marine life, including colorful fish, sea fans, and the occasional sea turtle.

- Cane Bay: In addition to its world-famous wall, Cane Bay offers fantastic snorkeling right from the beach. Explore the shallow reefs and seagrass beds, where you can spot parrotfish, angelfish, and other vibrant marine creatures.

Kayaking: Paddle Through Paradise

Kayaking in St. Croix is a serene yet exhilarating way to explore the island's coastal beauty and hidden coves.

- Bioluminescent Bay: Experience the magic of kayaking in a bioluminescent bay, where the water glows with ethereal blue light. This natural phenomenon is caused by microscopic organisms that emit light when disturbed. Paddle through the bay at night and watch as your movements create trails of shimmering light.

- Salt River Bay: Paddle through the tranquil waters of Salt River Bay, a historic and ecologically significant area. Explore the mangrove forests, spot wildlife like herons and iguanas, and learn about the area's rich history as you glide through this serene environment.

- West End Waters: For a more adventurous kayaking experience, head to the west end of the island, where you can paddle along rugged coastlines, explore hidden sea caves, and enjoy breathtaking views of the Caribbean Sea.

Hiking: Trails with a View

St. Croix's diverse landscapes offer excellent hiking opportunities, with trails that lead you through lush forests, along dramatic coastlines, and up to stunning viewpoints.

- The Annaly Bay Tide Pools: This moderately challenging hike takes you through the rainforest to the natural tide pools at Annaly Bay. The pools are formed by volcanic rock and offer a refreshing reward at the end of your hike. Take a dip in the clear waters and enjoy the beautiful coastal views.

- Mount Eagle: For panoramic views of the island, hike to the summit of Mount Eagle, the highest point on St. Croix. The trail winds through tropical forests and offers breathtaking vistas of the island and the surrounding Caribbean Sea.

- Jack and Isaac Bay Preserve: This scenic trail on the east end of the island takes you through a nature preserve to two of St. Croix's most pristine beaches. The hike offers stunning views of the coastline and the opportunity to spot native wildlife.

Water Sports: Ride the Waves

If you're looking for high-octane adventure, St. Croix's water sports scene won't disappoint.

- Windsurfing and Kitesurfing: The consistent trade winds and clear waters make St. Croix a paradise for windsurfing and kitesurfing. Head to areas like Southgate Coastal Reserve or Rainbow Beach to catch the best winds and ride the waves.

- Jet Skiing: For a thrilling ride, rent a jet ski and zip across the turquoise waters of the Caribbean Sea. Several beachside operators offer jet ski rentals and guided tours, allowing you to explore the island's coastline at high speed.

- Stand-Up Paddleboarding (SUP): For a more relaxed yet engaging water activity, try stand-up paddleboarding. Glide across the calm waters, explore hidden coves, and get a unique perspective of the island's marine life.

St. Croix's adventure activities offer endless opportunities to explore, discover, and thrill your senses. Whether you're diving into the depths of the Caribbean Sea, snorkeling vibrant coral reefs, paddling through glowing waters, or hiking to breathtaking viewpoints, each adventure promises unforgettable moments and a deeper connection with the island's natural beauty. Embrace the adventure and let St. Croix's exhilarating activities create memories that will last a lifetime. Welcome to a world of endless excitement and exploration!

Chapter 6. Experiencing the Culture

Local Festivals and Events

St. Croix is not only a paradise of natural beauty but also a vibrant cultural hub where the island's rich heritage comes alive through its numerous festivals and events. These celebrations are a tapestry of music, dance, food, and community spirit, offering visitors a unique opportunity to immerse themselves in the island's culture and traditions. Here are some of the most captivating festivals and events that you must experience during your stay in St. Croix.

Crucian Christmas Festival: A Season of Joy

The Crucian Christmas Festival is the island's most anticipated and grandest celebration, spanning several weeks from December to January. This festival is a vibrant showcase of St. Croix's cultural diversity and community spirit, blending African, European, and Caribbean traditions in a spectacular array of events.

- Parades: The festival features two major parades— the Children's Parade and the Adults' Parade. These colorful processions are filled with dazzling costumes, lively music, and exuberant dancers, creating a carnival-like atmosphere that fills the streets of Frederiksted with joy and excitement.

- Food Fair: Indulge in local delicacies at the food fair, where vendors offer an array of traditional dishes such as kallaloo, conch fritters, and johnnycakes. The fair is a feast for the senses, with the tantalizing aromas and flavors of Crucian cuisine drawing in crowds.

- Calypso and Soca Competitions: Enjoy electrifying performances by local artists competing in calypso and soca music contests. The infectious rhythms and spirited lyrics of these Caribbean music styles will have you dancing and singing along with the locals.

Emancipation Day: A Historic Celebration

Emancipation Day, celebrated on July 3rd, commemorates the abolition of slavery in the Danish West Indies (now the U.S. Virgin Islands) in 1848. This significant day is marked by events that honor the island's history and the resilience of its people.

- Ceremonies and Reenactments: Attend moving ceremonies and historical reenactments that tell the story of emancipation and pay tribute to the courage of those who fought for freedom. These events are both educational and inspiring, offering a profound connection to St. Croix's past.

- Cultural Performances: Experience traditional music, dance, and storytelling that celebrate the island's cultural heritage. These performances provide a deeper understanding of the cultural influences that have shaped St. Croix.

- Community Gatherings: Join locals in community gatherings and festivities that highlight the importance of unity and collective memory. Emancipation Day is a time of reflection, celebration, and communal pride.

Agrifest: A Celebration of Agriculture

The St. Croix Agricultural Fair, commonly known as Agrifest, is an annual event held in February that celebrates the island's agricultural heritage and showcases the best of local farming, crafts, and cuisine.

- Exhibitions and Competitions: Explore a wide range of exhibitions featuring livestock, produce, and agricultural products. Farmers and artisans compete for prizes, displaying their finest crops and handmade goods.

- Family-Friendly Activities: Agrifest offers fun activities for all ages, including petting zoos, pony rides, and educational workshops. It's a great way for families to learn about St. Croix's agricultural traditions and enjoy a day of wholesome entertainment.

- Food and Crafts: Sample delicious local food and browse unique crafts at the fair's many stalls. From fresh fruit and vegetables to handmade jewelry and souvenirs, Agrifest is a celebration of local talent and creativity.

St. Patrick's Day Parade: Island-Style Revelry

St. Patrick's Day in St. Croix is celebrated with a unique island twist, reflecting the island's diverse cultural influences. The parade, held in March in

Christiansted, is a lively and colorful event that attracts both locals and visitors.

- Parade Floats and Costumes: Marvel at the creative floats and festive costumes that fill the streets with green and gold. The parade is a joyous display of creativity and community spirit, with participants of all ages joining in the fun.

- Music and Dance: Enjoy live music and dance performances that blend Irish and Caribbean influences. The infectious rhythms and lively atmosphere make it impossible not to join in the revelry.

- Street Parties: After the parade, the celebration continues with street parties, where you can mingle with locals, enjoy delicious food and drinks, and dance the night away.

Crucian Carnival: A Cultural Extravaganza

Crucian Carnival, celebrated in July, is another major cultural event that showcases the island's vibrant traditions and festive spirit. This carnival is a kaleidoscope of colors, sounds, and flavors, offering an unforgettable experience for visitors.

- Costume Parades: The carnival features spectacular parades with participants dressed in elaborate costumes, reflecting various themes and cultural influences. The creativity and craftsmanship of these costumes are truly awe-inspiring.

- Music and Dance: Experience the infectious energy of calypso, soca, and reggae music, with live performances and dance competitions that keep the festivities going day and night.

- Village Celebrations: The carnival village is the heart of the celebrations, with food stalls, craft vendors, and entertainment for all ages. It's a place where the community comes together to celebrate their shared heritage and joy.

St. Croix's local festivals and events are more than just celebrations—they are a reflection of the island's rich cultural tapestry and the enduring spirit of its people. Participating in these vibrant festivities allows you to experience the heart and soul of St. Croix, forging connections and creating memories that will last a lifetime. Embrace the festive spirit and let the island's cultural rhythms captivate your heart. Welcome to a celebration of life, community, and heritage

Arts and Crafts: Galleries and Studios

St. Croix is a haven for artists and craftspeople, where the island's natural beauty and rich cultural heritage inspire a vibrant and diverse arts scene. From charming galleries to unique studios, exploring St. Croix's arts and crafts scene offers visitors a chance to connect with the island's creative spirit and take home a piece of its beauty. Here are some of the must-visit galleries and studios that showcase the artistic talents of St. Croix.

The Caribbean Museum Center for the Arts: A Cultural Hub

 Located in the historic town of Frederiksted, the Caribbean Museum Center for the Arts (CMCArts) is a cornerstone of St. Croix's artistic community. This dynamic cultural hub hosts rotating exhibitions, workshops, and events that celebrate the island's diverse artistic expressions.

- Exhibitions: Wander through the museum's galleries, where you'll find thought-provoking exhibitions featuring works by local and regional artists. From contemporary paintings and sculptures to traditional crafts, the exhibits offer a broad spectrum of artistic styles and themes.

- Workshops and Classes: CMCArts offers a variety of workshops and classes for all ages, allowing visitors to engage with the creative process. Whether you're interested in pottery, painting, or photography, there's an opportunity to learn and create alongside talented artists.

- Cultural Events: The center also hosts cultural events, including musical performances, film screenings, and literary readings, providing a rich tapestry of artistic experiences that reflect the island's cultural diversity.

Art @ Top Hat: An Artistic Treasure Trove

 Nestled in the heart of Christiansted, Art @ Top Hat is a charming gallery that showcases the works of some of St. Croix's most talented artists. The gallery, housed in a historic building, offers an intimate setting for discovering the island's artistic treasures.

- Local Art: Explore a diverse collection of paintings, sculptures, ceramics, and jewelry created by local artists. Each piece reflects the unique perspectives and inspirations drawn from the island's landscapes, culture, and history.

- Meet the Artists: The gallery often hosts events where visitors can meet the artists, learn about their creative processes, and gain a deeper appreciation for their work. These interactions provide a personal connection to the art and the stories behind it.

- Unique Souvenirs: Art @ Top Hat also offers a selection of handmade crafts and souvenirs, making it the perfect place to find a special keepsake to remember your visit to St. Croix.

Mitchell Larsen Studio: A Legacy of Craftsmanship

For over 25 years, Mitchell Larsen Studio has been a beloved institution on St. Croix, known for its exquisite glasswork and fine craftsmanship. Located in Christiansted, the studio offers visitors a chance to see master artisans at work and purchase beautiful, one-of-a-kind pieces.

- Handcrafted Glassware: The studio is renowned for its handcrafted glassware, including vibrant sun catchers, delicate ornaments, and stunning jewelry. Each piece is meticulously crafted, reflecting the skill and creativity of the artisans.

- Studio Tours: Take a tour of the studio to see the glassblowing process in action. Watching the artisans shape molten glass into intricate designs is a mesmerizing experience that highlights the artistry and precision involved in this traditional craft.

- Custom Orders: Mitchell Larsen Studio also offers custom orders, allowing you to commission a unique piece that captures your personal taste and the essence of St. Croix.

Maria Henle Studio: Capturing the Island's Beauty

The Maria Henle Studio, located in a picturesque setting overlooking Christiansted Harbor, is dedicated to the work of the late Maria Henle, a celebrated photographer and artist whose legacy continues to inspire. The studio showcases her evocative photography, which captures the natural beauty and cultural richness of St. Croix.

- Photography Exhibits: Browse through stunning black-and-white and color photographs that document the island's landscapes, architecture, and people. Henle's work offers a timeless perspective on St. Croix, preserving moments of beauty and significance.

- Art and Books: In addition to photography, the studio offers a selection of art prints, books, and postcards featuring Henle's work. These items make wonderful gifts and souvenirs, allowing you to share the island's beauty with others.

- Artistic Legacy: The studio also highlights the artistic legacy of the Henle family, including works by Maria's father, painter Hans Henle, and sister, ceramicist Elsa Henle. This multi-generational collection showcases the enduring artistic talent within the family.

IB Designs: A Fusion of Art and Jewelry

 IB Designs, located in Christiansted, is a unique gallery and studio that specializes in handcrafted jewelry inspired by the island's natural beauty and cultural heritage. The studio's creations are a fusion of art and craftsmanship, resulting in pieces that are both elegant and meaningful.

- Handmade Jewelry: Discover a stunning array of jewelry, from intricate silver bracelets and necklaces to bold, colorful earrings. Each piece is handmade, reflecting the island's natural elements such as sea life, flowers, and tropical landscapes.

- Meet the Designer: The studio's founder and designer, Whealan Massicott, often works on-site, providing visitors with an opportunity to see the creative process and discuss the inspiration behind the designs. This personal interaction adds a special touch to your shopping experience.

- Custom Creations: IB Designs also offers custom jewelry services, allowing you to create a personalized piece that embodies your connection to St. Croix.

'Exploring the arts and crafts of St. Croix is a journey into the heart and soul of the island. Each gallery and studio offers a unique window into the creativity and passion of its artists, providing an enriching and inspiring experience. Whether you're admiring a beautiful painting, watching a glassblower at work, or selecting a piece of handmade jewelry, you'll find that St. Croix's artistic community is as warm and welcoming as the island itself. Immerse yourself in the creativity of St. Croix, and take home a piece of its artistic legacy. Welcome to a world where art and culture flourish.

Music and Dance: Feel the Rhythm

In St. Croix, music and dance are more than just forms of entertainment—they are integral to the island's cultural identity and a vital expression of its vibrant spirit. The rhythms of St. Croix are infused with a rich blend of African, European, and Caribbean influences, creating a unique and captivating soundscape that resonates deeply with both locals and visitors. When you immerse yourself in the music and dance of St. Croix, you not only feel the rhythm but also connect with the heartbeat of the island itself.

Calypso and Soca: The Sound of Celebration

Calypso and soca music are the lifeblood of St. Croix's festive atmosphere, especially during the island's numerous celebrations and festivals.

- Calypso: Originating from Trinidad and Tobago, calypso music has found a vibrant home in St. Croix. Known for its witty and often satirical lyrics, calypso tells stories of everyday life, politics, and social issues with a rhythmic and melodic flair. Local calypso competitions are a highlight of the Crucian Christmas Festival, where talented artists perform their catchy tunes to enthusiastic crowds.

- Soca: A faster-paced, dance-oriented genre, soca music gets everyone on their feet with its infectious beats and energetic vibes. Soca is a staple at street parties, parades, and carnival events, where the lively rhythms and high-energy performances create an atmosphere of pure joy and celebration.

Reggae and Dancehall: Island Vibes

St. Croix's music scene wouldn't be complete without the soulful sounds of reggae and the pulsating beats of dancehall. These genres, deeply rooted in Jamaican culture, have become integral parts of the island's musical landscape.

- Reggae: With its smooth, laid-back rhythms and powerful messages of love, peace, and social justice, reggae music resonates deeply with the people of St. Croix. Local reggae bands and artists often perform at beach bars, open-air concerts, and cultural festivals, offering a perfect backdrop for relaxing and enjoying the island vibes.

- Dancehall: For those who love to dance, the energetic and rhythmic beats of dancehall music provide the perfect soundtrack. Dancehall parties on the island are lively events where locals and visitors come together to dance the night away, showcasing impressive moves and infectious enthusiasm.

Quelbe: The Heartbeat of St. Croix

Quelbe, also known as "scratch band music," is the traditional folk music of the Virgin Islands and a cherished cultural treasure of St. Croix.

- Traditional Instruments: Quelbe music features unique instruments such as the banjo, guitar, conga drums, and the "scratch" or gourd, which gives the genre its distinctive sound. The rhythms are upbeat and lively, often accompanied by playful and humorous lyrics that tell stories of island life.

- Cultural Heritage: Quelbe holds a special place in the hearts of the people of St. Croix, representing the island's cultural heritage and history. Performances can be experienced at cultural events, festivals, and community gatherings, where the joyful sounds of quelbe invite everyone to join in the dance.

Dance: Move to the Beat

Dance is an essential part of life on St. Croix, with styles and movements that reflect the island's diverse cultural influences. From traditional dances to modern styles, the dance scene in St. Croix is as dynamic and vibrant as the music itself.

- Quadrille: A traditional dance of African and European origins, the quadrille is a lively and elegant folk dance performed at cultural festivals and special events. Dancers, dressed in colorful costumes, move in intricate patterns to the upbeat rhythms of quelbe music.

- Soca and Reggae Dance: At parties, festivals, and street parades, you'll see locals and visitors alike moving to the energetic beats of soca and reggae music. The dances are free-spirited and joyful, often involving group participation and spontaneous choreography.

- Modern Dance: St. Croix also embraces contemporary dance styles, with local dance troupes and schools offering performances and classes in genres such as hip-hop, ballet, and modern dance. These performances showcase the versatility and creativity of the island's dancers.

Live Music Venues: Where the Rhythm Comes Alive

To fully experience the musical pulse of St. Croix, visit some of the island's live music venues where local talent shines and the rhythms come alive.

- Beach Bars: Many of the island's beach bars feature live music, providing the perfect setting to enjoy the sounds of the island with your toes in the sand and a refreshing drink in hand. Places like Rhythms at Rainbow Beach and The Deep End Bar & Grill are popular spots to catch live performances.

- Cultural Festivals: During festivals and cultural events, live music fills the air, creating an atmosphere of celebration and community. From the Crucian Christmas Festival to the St. Patrick's Day Parade, these events offer numerous opportunities to experience the island's musical heritage.

- Local Nightclubs: For those who love to dance, St. Croix's nightclubs and dance halls are the places to be. Venues like Club Comanche and The Mill Harbour Condos often host live bands and DJs, keeping the dance floor packed and the energy high.

In St. Croix, music and dance are not just forms of entertainment—they are expressions of the island's soul. From the infectious beats of calypso and soca to the soulful sounds of reggae and the traditional rhythms of quelbe, the music of St. Croix invites you to feel the rhythm and embrace the island's vibrant culture. Whether you're dancing at a beach bar, swaying to the sounds of a live band, or participating in a cultural festival, the music and dance of St. Croix will leave an indelible mark on your heart. Let the rhythm of the island move you and become a part of the joyous celebration that is St. Croix. Welcome to a world where the beat never stops and the dance floor is always open—welcome to St. Croix.

Chapter 7. Food and Dining

Must-Try Dishes: A Culinary Journey

St. Croix is a paradise not only for its stunning landscapes and vibrant culture but also for its rich and diverse culinary scene. The island's cuisine is a delightful blend of Caribbean, African, European, and American influences, offering a gastronomic adventure that will tantalize your taste buds and leave you craving more. Embark on this culinary journey and discover the must-try dishes that define the flavors of St. Croix.

Kallaloo: A Hearty Tradition

Kallaloo is a quintessential dish of the Virgin Islands, a thick and flavorful stew that embodies the island's culinary heritage.

- Ingredients: This hearty dish is made from a variety of leafy greens such as spinach, okra, and watercress, simmered with meat or seafood—often including crab, conch, or saltfish. The stew is seasoned with local herbs and spices, creating a rich, savory flavor profile.

- Cultural Significance: Kallaloo is traditionally prepared for special occasions and family gatherings, symbolizing unity and celebration. Sharing a bowl of kallaloo is a way to experience the warmth and hospitality of Crucian culture.

- Where to Try: Many local restaurants, such as Harvey's in Christiansted, serve up delicious bowls of kallaloo. Be sure to try it with a side of fungi, a cornmeal-based accompaniment that pairs perfectly with the stew.

Pates: A Taste of the Caribbean

Pates (pronounced pah-tays) are a beloved snack in St. Croix, offering a tasty and convenient way to enjoy the island's flavors.

- Description: Pates are deep-fried pastries filled with a variety of savory ingredients, including spiced ground beef, chicken, saltfish, or vegetables. The crispy exterior and flavorful filling make them a satisfying treat any time of day.

- Street Food Delight: Often sold by street vendors and local bakeries, pates are a popular grab-and-go snack for both locals and visitors. Their portability and deliciousness make them a perfect bite to enjoy while exploring the island.

- Where to Try: Visit local spots like Singh's Fast Food or the La Reine Chicken Shack to sample some of the best pates on the island. Pair them with a refreshing local beverage like maubi or sorrel for an authentic experience.

Conch Fritters: Island Appetizers

Conch fritters are a staple appetizer in St. Croix, offering a delicious introduction to the island's seafood bounty.

- Ingredients: These savory fritters are made from conch meat—known for its tender and slightly sweet flavor—mixed with a batter of flour, herbs, and spices, then deep-fried to golden perfection.

- Dipping Sauces: Conch fritters are often served with tangy dipping sauces, such as aioli or a spicy Caribbean pepper sauce, adding an extra layer of flavor to each bite.

- Where to Try: Many beachside bars and restaurants, including Duggan's Reef and Rhythms at Rainbow

Beach, serve up delectable conch fritters that are perfect for enjoying with an ocean view.

Johnnycakes: A Comforting Classic

Johnnycakes are a traditional Caribbean comfort food that holds a special place in the hearts (and stomachs) of the people of St. Croix.

- Description: These fluffy, slightly sweet cornmeal cakes are fried until golden brown and can be enjoyed plain or with various toppings such as butter, jam, or local honey.

- Versatility: Johnnycakes are often served as a side dish with savory meals or as a breakfast item. Their simple yet satisfying flavor makes them a beloved staple in Crucian cuisine.

- Where to Try: Experience the best johnnycakes at local eateries like The Breakfast Club or The

Courtyard, where they are made fresh daily and served with a side of island hospitality.

Roti: A Caribbean Classic

Roti, a dish with East Indian origins, has become a favorite in St. Croix, reflecting the island's diverse cultural influences.

- Description: Roti consists of a soft, flaky flatbread wrapped around a filling of curried meat or vegetables. Common fillings include chicken, goat, shrimp, and potatoes, all seasoned with a blend of aromatic spices.

- Flavor Explosion: The combination of tender, flavorful filling and warm, pillowy bread makes roti a satisfying and comforting meal that is perfect for any time of day.

- Where to Try: Head to Singh's Fast Food or Ital in Paradise to enjoy some of the best roti on the island.

These eateries are known for their authentic and mouthwatering versions of this Caribbean classic.

Tamarind Balls: A Sweet Treat

Tamarind balls are a popular sweet treat in St. Croix, offering a unique and tangy flavor that is sure to delight your taste buds.

- Ingredients: These chewy candies are made from tamarind pulp mixed with sugar and rolled into bite-sized balls, often coated with additional sugar for a sweet finish.

- Flavor Profile: The tartness of the tamarind combined with the sweetness of the sugar creates a perfect balance, making tamarind balls a refreshing and addictive snack.

- Where to Try: Look for tamarind balls at local markets and roadside stands. They are also often available in souvenir shops, making them a great gift to take home.

Bush Tea: A Traditional Beverage

Bush tea is a traditional herbal tea made from a variety of local plants and herbs, offering a soothing and healthful beverage experience.

- Ingredients: Common ingredients for bush tea include lemongrass, basil, mint, and soursop leaves, each imparting its own unique flavor and health benefits.

- Cultural Significance: Bush tea has been enjoyed by generations of Crucians for its medicinal properties and comforting taste. It is often consumed in the morning or evening as a calming ritual.

- Where to Try: Many local cafes and restaurants serve freshly brewed bush tea. For an authentic experience, visit the La Reine Farmers Market, where you can purchase dried herbs to brew your own tea at home.

St. Croix's culinary scene is a vibrant reflection of its diverse cultural heritage, offering a rich tapestry of flavors and traditions. From hearty stews and savory snacks to sweet treats and refreshing beverages, each dish tells a story of the island's history and the people who call it home. As you embark on this culinary journey, let your taste buds guide you through the island's rich gastronomic landscape, savoring each bite and sip along the way. Welcome to a world of flavors—welcome to the culinary heart of St. Croix.

Best Restaurants and Cafes

St. Croix's culinary scene is a melting pot of flavors, offering a delightful array of dining experiences that reflect the island's rich cultural heritage. From upscale restaurants serving gourmet cuisine to charming cafes offering local delicacies, the island's eateries promise to tantalize your taste buds and provide unforgettable dining moments. Here are some of the best restaurants and cafes in St. Croix that you must visit on your culinary journey.

The Terrace at The Buccaneer: Elegance and Ambiance

 Nestled within the luxurious Buccaneer Resort, The Terrace offers a dining experience that combines elegance with breathtaking views of the Caribbean Sea.

- Cuisine: The Terrace specializes in contemporary American cuisine with a Caribbean twist, featuring fresh, locally sourced ingredients. Signature dishes include grilled mahi-mahi, succulent steaks, and creative vegetarian options.

- Ambiance: With its open-air setting and panoramic ocean views, dining at The Terrace is an experience to remember. The warm, inviting atmosphere is perfect for a romantic dinner or a special celebration.
- Must-Try: Don't miss their famous breakfast buffet, where you can enjoy tropical fruits, pastries, and made-to-order omelets while taking in the stunning sunrise over the sea.

Savant: An Eclectic Culinary Adventure

Savant, located in the heart of Christiansted, is renowned for its eclectic menu and intimate, candlelit ambiance.

- Cuisine: Savant's menu is a fusion of Caribbean, Asian, and American flavors. The dishes are imaginative and beautifully presented, with popular options including the coconut curry mussels, jerk pork tenderloin, and their legendary fish tacos.

- Ambiance: The restaurant's cozy, bohemian decor creates a relaxed and romantic atmosphere. The charming courtyard, adorned with twinkling lights and lush greenery, adds to the restaurant's unique appeal.

- Must-Try: Indulge in their house-made desserts, especially the decadent chocolate mousse and the refreshing key lime pie.

Rhythms at Rainbow Beach: Casual Beachside Dining

For a laid-back dining experience with your toes in the sand, head to Rhythms at Rainbow Beach. This beachfront bar and grill is a favorite among locals and visitors alike.

- Cuisine: Rhythms offers a variety of Caribbean and American dishes, with an emphasis on fresh seafood and grilled meats. Popular choices include the conch fritters, fish tacos, and their mouthwatering burgers.
- Ambiance: The casual, beachside setting makes Rhythms the perfect spot to enjoy a meal while soaking up the sun and the island vibes. Live music and stunning sunsets add to the restaurant's vibrant atmosphere.
- Must-Try: Don't miss their famous "Lime in the Coconut" drink—a refreshing blend of coconut rum, fresh lime juice, and coconut cream.

117

Polly's at the Pier: A Charming Café Experience

Located in Frederiksted, Polly's at the Pier is a charming café that offers delicious food and a welcoming atmosphere.

- Cuisine: Polly's serves up a delightful selection of breakfast and lunch options, including fresh pastries, sandwiches, and salads. Their menu also features vegan and gluten-free options, catering to a variety of dietary preferences.
- Ambiance: The café's cozy interior and picturesque waterfront location make it a perfect spot to relax and enjoy a leisurely meal. The friendly staff and laid-back vibe add to the overall charm.
- Must-Try: Treat yourself to their freshly baked quiches and homemade iced teas, perfect for a light and satisfying meal.

St. Croix's culinary landscape is a feast for the senses, offering a diverse array of dining experiences that cater to every palate. From elegant fine dining establishments to charming beachside cafes, the island's restaurants showcase the rich flavors and vibrant culture of St. Croix. As you explore the island's culinary offerings, let each meal be a journey of discovery, delighting in the creativity and passion that define St. Croix's food scene. Welcome to a world of gastronomic pleasures—welcome to the dining paradise of St. Croix.

Chapter 8. Outdoor Adventures

Hiking Trails and Nature Walks

St. Croix, with its lush landscapes and stunning vistas, offers a wealth of opportunities for nature enthusiasts and adventure seekers. Hiking trails and nature walks on this enchanting island provide a perfect way to immerse yourself in its natural beauty, discover hidden gems, and experience the serenity of the great outdoors.

Lace up your hiking boots and get ready to explore some of the most captivating trails and nature walks that St. Croix has to offer.

The Annaly Bay Tide Pools: A Coastal Marvel

One of St. Croix's most popular hikes, the trail to the Annaly Bay Tide Pools, promises adventure and breathtaking coastal views.

- Trail Details: The hike starts at <u>Carambola Golf Club</u> and winds through the lush rainforest before descending to the rocky coastline. The trail is moderately challenging, with some steep sections, but the reward is well worth the effort.

- Highlights: Along the way, you'll encounter diverse flora and fauna, including tropical birds and vibrant flowers. The real highlight, however, is reaching the natural tide pools, where you can take a refreshing dip in crystal-clear waters while enjoying the stunning ocean views.

- Emotional Connection: As you traverse this trail, you'll feel a sense of connection with the island's raw and untouched beauty. The rhythmic sound of waves crashing against the rocks and the invigorating sea breeze will leave you feeling rejuvenated and inspired.

Jack and Isaac Bay Preserve: A Hidden Paradise

For those seeking tranquility and unspoiled beauty, the hike to Jack and Isaac Bay Preserve offers an unforgettable experience.

- Trail Details: This relatively easy hike begins at the east end of the island, near Point Udall. The trail is well-marked and takes you through dry forest and coastal terrain, eventually leading to the pristine beaches of Jack and Isaac Bay.

- Highlights: These secluded bays are protected as part of a nature preserve, providing a sanctuary for endangered sea turtles and a variety of marine life. Snorkeling in the clear, calm waters reveals a vibrant underwater world, while the pristine sandy beaches invite you to relax and soak in the sun.

- Emotional Connection: Walking this trail, you'll be enveloped by a profound sense of peace and solitude. The untouched beauty of the bays, the gentle lapping of waves, and the sight of sea turtles gliding gracefully through the water create a meditative and soul-nourishing experience.

The Rainforest of St. Croix: A Verdant Oasis

The western part of St. Croix is home to a lush tropical rainforest, offering a refreshing escape into nature's embrace.

- Trail Details: Several trails meander through the rainforest, with varying degrees of difficulty. One popular option is the trail leading to the Montpellier Domino Club, where you can enjoy a cool drink and meet the famous beer-drinking pigs.

- Highlights: The rainforest is a haven for biodiversity, with towering mahogany trees, vibrant orchids, and a chorus of bird calls creating a magical atmosphere. Along the trails, you might spot colorful parrots, shy deer, and playful mongoose.

- Emotional Connection: As you wander through the verdant canopy, you'll feel a deep sense of wonder and awe at the richness of nature. The cool, shaded paths and the earthy scent of the forest floor provide a sensory experience that calms the mind and uplifts the spirit.

Hams Bluff Lighthouse: A Journey Through History

The hike to Hams Bluff Lighthouse offers a blend of natural beauty and historical intrigue, making it a must-visit for history buffs and nature lovers alike.

- Trail Details: The trailhead is located near the northwest tip of the island, and the hike is relatively short but steep in sections. The path leads through dense vegetation and rocky terrain before reaching the lighthouse.

- Highlights: The historic lighthouse, perched on a cliff, offers panoramic views of the north shore and the Caribbean Sea. The dramatic cliffs and crashing waves below add to the sense of adventure and discovery.

- Emotional Connection: Standing at the base of the lighthouse, you'll feel a sense of connection to St. Croix's maritime history and the rugged beauty of its coastline. The expansive ocean views and the timeless presence of the lighthouse evoke feelings of nostalgia and admiration for the island's enduring spirit.

Hiking trails and nature walks on St. Croix offer more than just exercise—they provide an opportunity to connect with the island's soul. Each trail, with its unique landscapes and hidden wonders, invites you to explore and appreciate the diverse beauty of St. Croix.

As you embark on these outdoor adventures, you'll discover not only the physical beauty of the island but also a deeper sense of peace, inspiration, and belonging. Welcome to a world where every step leads to new discoveries and every moment in nature becomes a cherished memory. Welcome to the wild heart of St. Croix.

Water Sports: Sailing, Kayaking, and Paddleboarding

St. Croix is a haven for water sports enthusiasts, offering a playground of crystal-clear waters, gentle breezes, and stunning coastal scenery. Whether you're an experienced sailor, a casual kayaker, or a first-time paddleboarder, the island's vibrant marine environment promises adventure, excitement, and tranquility. Dive into the heart of St. Croix's water sports scene and discover the thrilling experiences that await you.

Sailing: Embrace the Open Sea

Sailing around St. Croix offers an unparalleled way to experience the island's beauty from a unique perspective.

- The Experience: Feel the wind in your hair and the salt spray on your skin as you navigate the turquoise waters of the Caribbean. St. Croix's favorable winds and calm seas create perfect conditions for both leisurely cruises and exhilarating sailing adventures.

- Highlights: Explore hidden coves, secluded beaches, and uninhabited islands. One popular destination is Buck Island, a protected national monument known for its spectacular underwater snorkel trail and pristine beaches.

- Emotional Connection: Sailing on St. Croix isn't just about the destination—it's about the journey. The rhythmic motion of the boat, the expansive horizon, and the symphony of wind and waves combine to create a sense of freedom and connection to nature that is profoundly soothing and invigorating.

Kayaking: Explore at Your Own Pace

Kayaking offers a serene and intimate way to explore St. Croix's coastline, mangroves, and inland waterways.

- The Experience: Glide silently through tranquil bays and winding mangrove channels, where you can get up close and personal with the island's rich marine life and diverse ecosystems. Kayaking allows you to explore areas that larger boats can't reach, providing a unique and peaceful adventure.

- Highlights: A must-try experience is a bioluminescent kayak tour in **Salt River Bay**. As night falls, the water comes alive with glowing microorganisms, creating a magical, otherworldly spectacle. Daytime kayaking adventures to places like

Green Cay and **Altona Lagoon** offer opportunities to spot sea turtles, stingrays, and colorful fish.

- Emotional Connection: The gentle rhythm of paddling and the quiet immersion in nature make kayaking a meditative and deeply satisfying experience. Whether you're exploring alone or with a companion, the sense of solitude and the beauty of the surroundings create moments of peace and reflection.

Paddleboarding: Balance and Bliss

Paddleboarding, with its blend of relaxation and exercise, has become a favorite activity for visitors and locals alike.

- The Experience: Stand-up paddleboarding (SUP) allows you to navigate the waters at your own pace, standing tall and taking in the panoramic views. It's a great way to combine physical fitness with the pleasure of being on the water.

- Highlights: Paddle along the calm waters of Frederiksted's west end, where you can enjoy the sunset from your board, or venture to Cane Bay for a morning paddle with the stunning backdrop of the north shore. Many local outfitters offer paddleboard rentals and guided tours, ensuring you have everything you need for a fantastic experience.

- Emotional Connection: The balance required for paddleboarding encourages a focus on the present moment, creating a mindful and grounding experience. The tranquility of floating on the water, coupled with the gentle exertion, brings a sense of harmony and well-being that stays with you long after you've returned to shore.

St. Croix's water sports opportunities are as varied as they are exhilarating. Whether you're slicing through the waves on a sailboat, exploring hidden nooks in a kayak, or finding your balance on a paddleboard, each activity offers a unique way to connect with the island's natural beauty.

The warm Caribbean waters, abundant marine life, and breathtaking landscapes provide a backdrop for adventures that are as thrilling as they are serene. As you embrace these water sports, you'll find yourself immersed in the rhythms of the sea, forging memories that are both exhilarating and deeply peaceful. Welcome to a world where every splash and ripple brings joy, discovery, and a profound connection to the stunning island of St. Croix.

Chapter 9. Shopping and Souvenirs

Local Crafts and Handmade Goods

St. Croix's vibrant culture and rich heritage come to life through its local crafts and handmade goods. The island is a treasure trove of unique, artisanal products that reflect the creativity and traditions of its people. As you wander through markets and boutiques, you'll discover an array of beautifully crafted items, each telling its own story. From intricate jewelry to handwoven textiles, exploring St. Croix's local crafts offers a meaningful connection to the island and its artisans.

Jewelry: Treasures from the Sea

One of the most distinctive and cherished crafts on St. Croix is its handmade jewelry, often inspired by the island's natural beauty and marine life.

- The Craft: Local artisans skillfully transform materials such as coral, shells, and sea glass into stunning pieces of jewelry. These materials, naturally polished by the ocean, are combined with metals like silver and gold to create unique necklaces, bracelets, and earrings.

- Where to Find: Visit Crucian Gold in Christiansted, a family-owned shop known for its handcrafted jewelry that captures the essence of the island. Their iconic "Crucian Knot" designs symbolize unity and strength, making for a perfect souvenir or gift.

- Emotional Connection: Wearing a piece of locally made jewelry not only adds a touch of St. Croix's beauty to your wardrobe but also serves as a reminder of your connection to the island's culture and natural surroundings.

Textiles and Fabrics: Weaving Stories

St. Croix's textile arts are a blend of traditional techniques and modern creativity, resulting in beautiful, functional pieces that are perfect for any home.

- The Craft: Artisans use various methods, including weaving, batik, and hand-painting, to create vibrant textiles. These techniques produce stunning scarves, tablecloths, and other fabric items adorned with tropical motifs and vivid colors.

- Where to Find: Seek out local markets like the Christiansted Boardwalk or Frederiksted's Saturday Market, where you can meet artisans and purchase their handcrafted textiles directly. The St. Croix Educational Complex also offers a range of beautifully woven and batik items.

- Emotional Connection: Each textile piece tells a story through its patterns and colors, reflecting the island's landscapes and cultural heritage. Owning a handmade fabric item allows you to bring a piece of St. Croix's artistry and warmth into your home.

Pottery and Ceramics: Island Artistry

The pottery and ceramics of St. Croix showcase the island's artistic talent and creativity, resulting in functional art that adds a unique touch to any space.

- The Craft: Local potters use traditional techniques to create beautiful ceramics, including bowls, mugs, and decorative items. The designs often feature tropical themes and vibrant glazes that capture the essence of the island.

- Where to Find: Visit The Caribbean Museum Center for the Arts in Frederiksted, which hosts exhibitions and sells works by local ceramic artists. You can also explore various galleries and studios around the island, such as ib designs in Christiansted.

- Emotional Connection: Handmade ceramics bring the island's spirit into your daily life, whether you're sipping coffee from a handcrafted mug or displaying a beautifully glazed bowl. These items serve as functional reminders of the island's creativity and charm.

Handmade Soaps and Candles: Scented Memories

Bring the scents of St. Croix home with you through handmade soaps and candles, crafted with natural ingredients and infused with the island's aromas.

- The Craft: Local artisans use natural oils, herbs, and essential oils to create soaps and candles that evoke the island's tropical environment. Scents like coconut, lemongrass, and hibiscus transport you back to the island with every use.

- Where to Find: Check out local shops like ib designs and island markets for these fragrant products. The unique blends and high-quality ingredients make for thoughtful gifts and personal treats.

- Emotional Connection: Using handmade soaps and candles provides a sensory experience that reminds you of St. Croix's natural beauty and relaxing atmosphere. The scents and textures offer a daily escape back to the island's tranquility.

Exploring the local crafts and handmade goods of St. Croix allows you to take home more than just a souvenir. Each piece is a work of art, imbued with the skill, creativity, and cultural heritage of the island's artisans. As you browse through markets and shops, you'll find items that speak to your heart and remind you of your time on this beautiful island. These handmade treasures offer a tangible connection to St. Croix, letting you carry a piece of its soul with you, wherever you go.

Duty-Free Shopping: What to Buy

St. Croix is a paradise for shoppers, especially when it comes to duty-free shopping. The island offers a range of products at tax-free prices, making it an ideal destination for those looking to indulge in some retail therapy. Whether you're seeking luxury items, local crafts, or unique souvenirs, duty-free shopping in St. Croix promises exceptional deals and a delightful shopping experience. Here's a guide to what you should buy to make the most of your duty-free privileges.

Jewelry and Watches: Sparkling Savings

St. Croix is renowned for its exquisite jewelry stores, where you can find dazzling pieces at unbeatable prices.

- What to Buy: Look for fine jewelry featuring diamonds, emeralds, and other precious stones. High-end watches from brands like Rolex, Omega, and Tag Heuer are also available at significant discounts.

- Where to Shop: Christiansted and Frederiksted are home to several reputable jewelry stores, including IB Designs and Sonya's, famous for their original "hook" bracelets. The Christiansted Boardwalk offers a variety of shops with stunning selections.

- Emotional Connection: Buying jewelry on St. Croix not only offers financial savings but also allows you to take home a beautiful piece that captures the island's charm and elegance. Each time you wear it, you'll be reminded of your time in paradise.

Perfumes and Cosmetics: Luxurious Fragrances

Indulge in high-end perfumes and cosmetics from renowned brands at duty-free prices, perfect for adding a touch of luxury to your daily routine.

- What to Buy: Perfumes from top brands like Chanel, Dior, and Lancôme, as well as premium cosmetics and skincare products.

- Where to Shop: Many of the island's boutiques and department stores carry a wide selection of fragrances and beauty products. Check out stores in Christiansted for the best variety.

- Emotional Connection: Scent is a powerful memory trigger. Selecting a new fragrance during your trip means that every time you wear it, the aroma will transport you back to the sun-soaked beaches and vibrant atmosphere of St. Croix.

Liquor and Spirits: Taste of the Tropics

Take advantage of duty-free prices on liquor and spirits, including some local favorites that offer a true taste of the Caribbean.

- What to Buy: Local rum is a must-buy. Brands like Cruzan Rum, distilled right on the island, offer a variety of flavors and blends that make perfect souvenirs or gifts. Other spirits, including whiskey, vodka, and gin, are also available at great prices.

- Where to Shop: Visit the Cruzan Rum Distillery for a tour and tasting, and purchase your favorite bottles directly from the source. Liquor stores and duty-free shops across the island also stock a wide range of spirits.

- Emotional Connection: Bringing home a bottle of local rum allows you to savor the flavors of St. Croix long after your trip. Sharing it with friends and family can bring a piece of your island adventure to them.

Cigars: Caribbean Craftsmanship

For cigar aficionados, St. Croix offers a selection of fine cigars that exemplify the art of Caribbean craftsmanship.

- What to Buy: Look for hand-rolled cigars made from high-quality tobacco. Local brands often provide a unique smoking experience that captures the essence of the Caribbean.

- Where to Shop: Specialty cigar shops in Christiansted and Frederiksted offer a variety of options. Some even have lounges where you can sample cigars before making your purchase.

- Emotional Connection: Smoking a hand-rolled cigar from St. Croix is more than just an indulgence—it's an experience that connects you to the island's tradition of craftsmanship and relaxation.

Electronics and Gadgets: High-Tech Deals

If you're in the market for the latest electronics, St. Croix's duty-free shops offer significant savings on a range of high-tech gadgets.

- What to Buy: Cameras, smartphones, tablets, and other electronic devices from leading brands.

- Where to Shop: Department stores and specialty electronics shops in Christiansted and Frederiksted.

- Emotional Connection: Bringing home a new gadget purchased on St. Croix not only saves you money but also gives you a practical reminder of your trip. Capture your vacation memories with a new camera or stay connected with a new smartphone.

Clothing and Accessories: Island Style

Update your wardrobe with stylish clothing and accessories that reflect the island's vibrant and laid-back lifestyle.

- What to Buy: Resort wear, beachwear, and accessories like hats and sunglasses. Look for unique pieces that showcase local designers and island-inspired fashions.

- Where to Shop: Boutiques and shops throughout Christiansted and Frederiksted offer a range of stylish options. Don't miss out on local markets where you can find handmade accessories and unique apparel.

- Emotional Connection: Wearing clothing and accessories bought on St. Croix allows you to carry a piece of the island's style with you, keeping the spirit of your vacation alive in your everyday life.

St. Croix's duty-free shopping offers an exciting and rewarding experience for every type of shopper. Whether you're looking for luxury items, local crafts, or practical gadgets, the island's stores provide excellent value and a diverse range of products. As you explore the shopping districts, you'll not only find great deals but also connect with the island's culture and creativity. Happy shopping, and may your purchases bring back fond memories of your unforgettable time in St. Croix!

Chapter 10. Practical Information

Currency and Banking: What to Know

Navigating currency and banking while traveling can often be a source of stress, but St. Croix makes it easy for visitors to manage their finances. With a straightforward banking system and a widely accepted currency, you'll find that handling money is a breeze on this beautiful island. Here's everything you need to know about currency and banking in St. Croix to ensure your trip is as smooth and enjoyable as possible.

Currency: The U.S. Dollar

St. Croix, as part of the U.S. Virgin Islands, uses the U.S. dollar (USD) as its official currency. This is a great convenience for travelers from the United States, as there's no need to worry about exchange rates or carrying foreign currency.

- What to Know: Bills are available in denominations of $1, $5, $10, $20, $50, and $100. Coins include pennies, nickels, dimes, and quarters.
- Emotional Connection: Knowing you can use the same currency simplifies your travel experience, letting you focus on enjoying the island's beauty and attractions without worrying about conversions or exchange fees.

Banking Services: Accessible and Convenient

St. Croix offers a range of banking services to ensure you can manage your money effortlessly during your stay.

- ATMs: Automated Teller Machines (ATMs) are widely available across the island, particularly in major towns like Christiansted and Frederiksted. They dispense U.S. dollars and accept most major credit and debit cards. Look for ATMs at banks, shopping centers, and even some larger hotels.

- Banks: Several banks operate on the island, including Banco Popular, FirstBank, and Bank of St. Croix. These banks offer a full range of services, including currency exchange, wire transfers, and account withdrawals.

- Emotional Connection: The availability of familiar banking services provides a sense of security and ease, allowing you to focus on the adventure and relaxation that St. Croix offers.

Using Credit and Debit Cards: Easy Transactions

Credit and debit cards are widely accepted on St. Croix, making transactions simple and convenient.

- What to Know: Major credit cards, including Visa, MasterCard, and American Express, are accepted at most hotels, restaurants, and shops. However, it's a good idea to carry some cash for smaller establishments or markets that may not accept cards.

- Emotional Connection: The ease of using your credit or debit card means you can dine, shop, and explore without the hassle of carrying large amounts of cash. This convenience enhances your overall travel experience, letting you enjoy the island's offerings worry-free.

Tips for Currency Exchange: Be Prepared

While the U.S. dollar is the official currency, visitors from other countries might need to exchange their home currency. Here are some tips to ensure a smooth exchange process.

- Before You Go: If you're traveling from outside the United States, consider exchanging some of your home currency for U.S. dollars before arriving in St. Croix. This can help you avoid high exchange fees and ensure you have cash on hand for immediate expenses.
- On the Island: Banks and some hotels offer currency exchange services. It's always wise to compare rates and fees before making an exchange.
- Emotional Connection: Being prepared with the right currency allows you to dive straight into your St. Croix adventure without unnecessary financial worries, ensuring you start your vacation on the right foot.

Practical Tips: Smooth Financial Transactions

Here are a few practical tips to keep your financial transactions smooth and stress-free while in St. Croix.

- Notify Your Bank: Inform your bank and credit card companies of your travel plans to avoid any security holds on your accounts due to unusual activity.
- Carry Some Cash: While cards are widely accepted, having some cash is useful for small purchases, tips, and in places where cards might not be accepted.
- Check Fees: Be aware of any international transaction fees that your bank might charge for using your card abroad, even though St. Croix uses U.S. currency.
- Keep Receipts: Save receipts of your transactions and withdrawals. They can be helpful for budgeting and in case of any discrepancies.

With the U.S. dollar as the official currency and a well-established banking system, handling money in St. Croix is straightforward and convenient. Whether you're using credit cards for dining and shopping or withdrawing cash from ATMs for smaller expenses, you'll find that managing your finances is one of the easiest parts of your trip. This financial ease allows you to focus on what truly matters: soaking in the stunning views, experiencing the rich culture, and making unforgettable memories on the beautiful island of St. Croix.

Language and Communication

Communication is key to fully experiencing and enjoying your time in St. Croix. Understanding the local language and customs can enrich your interactions and help you connect more deeply with the island's vibrant culture. Here's everything you need to know about language and communication to ensure a smooth and engaging stay on this beautiful Caribbean island.

English: The Official Language

St. Croix, as part of the U.S. Virgin Islands, has English as its official language. This makes communication straightforward for English-speaking visitors, allowing for easy navigation and interaction.

English is spoken by the vast majority of residents, making it the primary language for business, education, and daily conversation. You'll find that road signs, menus, and informational brochures are all in English.

Knowing that you can communicate in English removes any language barriers, allowing you to immerse yourself in the island's culture and engage more deeply with the people you meet.

Local Dialects: A Flavor of the Caribbean

While English is the official language, you might notice a distinct local dialect, often referred to as "Cruzan." This dialect adds a unique flavor to the language and reflects the island's rich cultural heritage.

Cruzan English incorporates elements of African, European, and Caribbean languages, resulting in a melodic and expressive way of speaking. You might hear phrases and idioms that are unique to the island.

Embracing the local dialect, even learning a few phrases, can endear you to the locals and provide a deeper appreciation of St. Croix's cultural tapestry. It's a way to show respect and connect on a more personal level.

Speak Like a Local

Learning a few common phrases can go a long way in enhancing your interactions and showing your appreciation for the local culture.

- Greetings: "Good day" is a common greeting that can be used throughout the day. "Good night" is often used as a greeting in the evening, not just a farewell.

- Politeness: Saying "please" and "thank you" (or "tank you" in the local dialect) is always appreciated. "Yes, please" and "No, thank you" are polite ways to respond in any situation.

Using these phrases shows that you're making an effort to respect and understand the local culture, which can lead to warmer interactions and a more enriching travel experience.

Digital Communication: Staying Connected

Staying connected in St. Croix is easy with the island's robust communication infrastructure. Whether you need to make a call, send a text, or access the internet, you'll find reliable services available.

- Cell Service: Major U.S. carriers like AT&T, Verizon, and T-Mobile offer coverage in St. Croix. Check with your provider about international roaming plans to avoid unexpected charges.

- Internet Access: Wi-Fi is widely available at hotels, restaurants, and public areas. Many businesses offer free Wi-Fi for customers, making it easy to stay connected.

Staying connected allows you to share your experiences in real-time, keeping loved ones updated on your adventures and helping you navigate your travel plans smoothly.

Practical Tips: Effective Communication

Here are a few practical tips to enhance your communication experience in St. Croix.

- Be Polite and Patient: Island life tends to be more laid-back and relaxed. Politeness and patience go a long way in making positive connections with locals.

- Listen and Learn: Pay attention to the local dialect and try to pick up on common phrases. Locals will appreciate your effort to understand and speak their way.

- Ask Questions: If you're unsure about something, don't hesitate to ask. Locals are generally friendly and willing to help, and asking questions can lead to interesting conversations and new insights.

Language and communication are vital parts of your travel experience, and in St. Croix, they are gateways to deeper connections and richer interactions. With English as the official language and a charming local dialect to explore, you'll find it easy to navigate conversations and engage with the island's warm and welcoming people. By embracing the local language and customs, you'll not only enhance your travel experience but also create lasting memories of your time in this Caribbean paradise.

Conclusion: What Makes St. Croix Special

St. Croix is more than just a tropical getaway; it's a vibrant tapestry of history, culture, natural beauty, and warm hospitality. Throughout this guide, we've explored the island's stunning beaches, rich historical landmarks, thrilling adventure activities, and unique local festivals. We've delved into the heart of St. Croix's culture, from its soulful music and dance to its intricate arts and crafts. We've savored the island's culinary delights and discovered the best spots for dining and shopping.

A Unique Blend of History and Culture

What truly sets St. Croix apart is its unique blend of history and culture. Walking through the cobblestone streets of Christiansted or Frederiksted, you can't help but feel the echoes of the past mingling with the vibrant present. The island's historical landmarks, such as Fort Christiansvaern and the Estate Whim Plantation Museum, offer a glimpse into a rich and complex history that has shaped the island into what it is today. The local festivals and events are not just celebrations but reflections of a community deeply connected to its roots and proud of its heritage.

Natural Beauty and Adventure

St. Croix's natural beauty is nothing short of breathtaking. From the pristine beaches of Sandy Point and Rainbow Beach to the lush, green trails of the Rainforest, every corner of the island invites exploration and adventure. Whether you're diving into the crystal-clear waters to explore coral reefs, kayaking through mangroves, or hiking up to scenic viewpoints, the island's landscapes offer endless opportunities for discovery and excitement. The serene beauty of St. Croix's natural environment is complemented by a plethora of outdoor activities, making it a paradise for adventure seekers and nature lovers alike.

Warmth and Hospitality

What makes St. Croix truly special is the warmth and hospitality of its people. The friendly smiles, welcoming greetings, and genuine kindness you'll encounter throughout your stay create an atmosphere of comfort and belonging. The island's residents are not just hosts but storytellers, eager to share their culture, traditions, and way of life with visitors. This warmth extends to every interaction, making your experience on the island feel more like a visit with old friends than a typical vacation.

St. Croix is a place that stays with you long after you've left its shores. It's in the memories of the sunset over the Caribbean Sea, the taste of freshly caught seafood, and the rhythm of calypso music that makes you tap your feet. It's in the handcrafted jewelry that reminds you of the artisans you met and the friendly conversations that made you feel at home. St. Croix isn't just a destination; it's a collection of moments and experiences that become part of your personal story.

Thank You and a Small Request

Thank you for choosing this guide to accompany you on your journey to St. Croix. I hope it has provided you with valuable insights, practical tips, and a deeper appreciation for this incredible island. Your adventure doesn't end here; the memories and connections you've made will continue to enrich your life.

If you found this guide helpful, please consider leaving a review. Your feedback not only helps other travelers but also allows me to improve and continue sharing the wonders of St. Croix with the world. Your experiences and insights are invaluable, and I would love to hear about your journey.

Safe travels, and may your time in St. Croix be filled with joy, discovery, and unforgettable moments.

To access other books in our library, scan the code above.

Made in United States
Troutdale, OR
12/17/2024

26771714R00096